30233
JB LEE / Robert E. Lee JBIOG

In Memory of
Tamara LaBonte
by
Greg & Liane Hammer
2001

FEB 2 4 2004	**DATE DUE**	

Robert
E. Lee

From his early heroics in the Mexican War to his startling string of victories as commander of the Confederate forces in the Civil War, Robert E. Lee was among the most outstanding military leaders in the history of the United States.

Junior ■ World ■ Biographies

Robert E. Lee

Jack Kavanagh and
Eugene C. Murdoch

CHELSEA JUNIORS
a division of CHELSEA HOUSE PUBLISHERS

English-language words that are italicized in the text can be found in the glossary at the back of the book.

Chelsea House Publishers

EDITORIAL DIRECTOR Richard Rennert
EXECUTIVE MANAGING EDITOR Karyn Gullen Browne
COPY CHIEF Robin James
PICTURE EDITOR Adrian G. Allen
ART DIRECTOR Robert Mitchell
MANUFACTURING DIRECTOR Gerald Levine

JUNIOR WORLD BIOGRAPHIES

SENIOR EDITOR Ann-Jeanette Campbell
SERIES DESIGN Marjorie Zaum

Staff for ROBERT E. LEE
ASSOCIATE EDITOR David Shirley
COPY EDITOR Joy Sanchez
EDITORIAL ASSISTANTS Kelsey Goss and Scott D. Briggs
PICTURE RESEARCHER Villette Harris
COVER ILLUSTRATION Robert Caputo

Copyright © 1995 by Chelsea House Publishers, a subsidiary of Haights Cross Communications. All rights reserved. Printed and bound in the United States of America.

3 5 7 9 8 6 4 2

Library of Congress Cataloging-in-Publication Data
Jack Kavanagh.
  Robert E. Lee / Jack Kavanagh and Eugene C. Murdoch.
    p. cm.—(Junior world biographies)
  Includes bibliographical references and index.
ISBN 0-7910-1768-0.
    0-7910-2143-2 (pbk.)
  1. Lee, Robert E. (Robert Edward), 1807–1870—Juvenile literature. 2. Generals—United States—Biography—Juvenile literature. 3. Generals—Confederate States of America —Biography—Juvenile literature.
4. United States. Army—Biography—Juvenile literature. 5. Confederate States of America. Army—Biography—Juvenile literature. I. Murdoch, Eugene C. II. Title. III. Series.
E467.1.L4K38 1994
973.7'3'092—dc20   94-14732
[B]   CIP
                                                                            AC

Contents

1	Before the War	7
2	Mexico and Beyond	19
3	Commanding the Army of Northern Virginia	35
4	The High Tide of the Confederacy	43
5	The Defeat of the South	53
6	After the War	65
	Further Reading	73
	Glossary	74
	Chronology	76
	Index	78

Confederate general Robert E. Lee hated slavery and opposed the Confederacy's defense of the practice. Lee's first allegiance, however, was to his native South and his home state of Virginia. When Confederate president Jefferson Davis invited Lee to command the Confederate army he quickly accepted.

CHAPTER

1
Before the War

Just after daybreak on April 12, 1861, the big guns of the new Confederate army began to boom. Their huge cannons bombarded Fort Sumter, the *Union* stronghold in the middle of the harbor at Charleston, South Carolina. The Rebels kept up the attack for two days. Finally, the *besieged* Federal garrison was forced to lower the flag. The Union's Stars and Stripes were taken down. The new flag of the Confederacy, the Stars and Bars, flew in its place. The new flag was to wave defiantly through four full years of rebellion and war. The Civil War had begun.

The nation had been divided for years over slavery. The war was a result of this conflict. The southern states used black people brought in chains from Africa to plant and harvest the cotton and tobacco crops. The more industrialized northern states had stopped using slaves, and they insisted that their southern neighbors do the same. As the United States expanded from the original 13 colonies, each new state had to decide whether to enter the Union as a "free state" or a "slave state."

Abraham Lincoln, the new president of the United States, had declared, "I believe this government cannot endure permanently half slave and half free." Thinking that Lincoln would end slavery, seven states in the Deep South *seceded* from the Union and formed their own government. They left the Union between December 1860 and February 1861, even before Lincoln was sworn in as president on March 4, 1861. The seven defiant states called themselves the Confederate

States of America and appealed to the other southern states to join them.

The most important of these undecided states was Virginia. Virginia was the state that had given America its first president, George Washington. Thomas Jefferson, James Madison, Patrick Henry, and the dashing hero of the American Revolution, "Light-Horse Harry" Lee, were all Virginians. Lee's son, Robert, of Arlington, Virginia, was the nation's outstanding fighting man as the nation now prepared itself for civil war.

Robert E. Lee dreaded the choice that he knew he would be forced to make if the northern and southern states went to war. He was a career soldier who served his country proudly. If forced to choose, however, he knew that he would remain a loyal Virginian. When the news of the firing on Fort Sumter reached Washington, D.C., on April 15, Lincoln ordered the raising of 75,000 volunteer troops to "suppress *insurrection* and rebellion."

The next day a message was delivered to Colonel Robert E. Lee. It came from the commanding general of the United States Army, Winfield Scott. Scott had been Lee's commander in the war with Mexico 15 years earlier. The aging warrior knew that he could not lead the Union armies in the field any longer, and he wanted his younger protégé to take command of all the Union armies. Sadly, Lee refused. He told his old commander that he could never fight against his own state of Virginia. Instead, he planned to resign his military *commission* and return to private life.

Lee did not remain a private citizen for long, however. Within a few days, he found himself in Richmond, the state capital of Virginia and the new capital of the Confederate States of America. To no one's surprise, Lee had been chosen to command the state's military forces.

Lee was 53 years old when Fort Sumter was shelled. He was born at the family home of Stratford Hall, in Westmoreland County, Virginia, in 1807. Robert was the fourth of five children. His

Though his life ended in poverty and disgrace, Henry Lee was a popular revolutionary war hero and a member of the U.S. Congress. The older Lee was also a good friend of George Washington, whom he honored with the now-famous epitaph, "first in war, first in peace and first in the hearts of his countrymen." The two men would serve as Robert's heroes throughout the younger Lee's early years in the military.

mother, Anne Carter Lee, was the daughter of one of the state's most *prominent* families. His father, Henry Lee, was a popular revolutionary war hero who went on to become the state governor and a member of the federal legislature. Light-Horse Harry Lee was a close friend of George Washington, and young Robert grew up with both men as his heroes.

Washington made a fine role model for a boy. Light-Horse Harry Lee did not. Lee's style in battle had been daring and colorful, but as a landowner, he was reckless and irresponsible. He wasted his family's fortune in foolish land investments. When he died, his son was only 11 years old and was forced to depend on his friends for his education.

Because his father had been a soldier, Robert wanted to go to the United States Military Academy. The prestigious academy had opened 20 years earlier, in West Point, New York, and it was difficult to gain admission to the *cadet* corps. Robert received recommendations from family friends, congressmen, and senators. People remembered that Robert's father had been a popular hero of the American Revolution. Lee finally entered the academy in the summer of 1825 with an appointment from the secretary of war, John C. Calhoun.

At the time, America was at peace. The young country's last battles had been fought more than a decade earlier in the War of 1812 against England. During peacetime, the academy trained its officers to be engineers. Mathematics and science courses were taught along with basic military skills. Lee was a good student from the beginning, and he graduated second in his class in 1829. He was 22 years old at the time, stood five feet ten inches tall, and weighed about 170 pounds. He was a good-looking man with thick, wavy black hair and, even at such a young age, carried himself with a dignified military bearing. Lee was well liked by all his classmates and commanding officers.

After graduation, Lee was ready to serve his country. But a bad blow awaited him when he

This portrait of Mary Custis Lee was painted around the time of her marriage to Robert E. Lee in 1831. Lee met Mary Custis while he was on furlough from West Point.

returned to his home in Virginia. His mother, who had been ill for some time, died soon after he reached Alexandria. Gripped by sorrow, Lee left for his first assignment as a military engineer. He was sent to a mosquito-infested, swampy island near Savannah, Georgia. His goal was to build a fort on nearby Cockspur Island. Lee turned out to be good at getting tough jobs done, and the army rewarded his skills by continually giving him its toughest and most demanding assignments. He spent most of his earlier years in the military traveling to rough, isolated areas to build forts and dams and to clear rivers and harbors. Later, when Lee finally began to receive combat assignments, he found that his knowledge of engineering gave him a great advantage over his enemies. Many important battles were won because Lee knew how to move troops and supplies effectively and keep a step ahead of the enemy.

Several years after graduating from West Point, Lee met Mary Custis, the adopted daughter of George Washington's adopted son, George Washington Parke Custis. Lee fell in love with the young woman at once. At first, Mary's parents were hesitant to allow their daughter to marry the young officer because of his father's tarnished reputation. But the young couple remained devoted to each other, and they were finally married on June 30, 1831, at the Custis family home on the banks of the Potomac River in Arlington, Virginia.

While Robert was away on various military assignments, Mary remained at the Custis estate, where she began to raise the first of the Lees' seven children. Although he was a devoted father, Lee was also a career army officer. He was often away from his three sons and four daughters during their childhood. At times, during the late 1830s and early 1840s, Lee served assignments in St. Louis, Missouri, and New York City that enabled him to spend much more time with his family. After clearing the waters of the Mississippi River and New York Harbor, however, Lee was ready to test his skills on the battlefield. Finally, in the summer of 1846, he was sent to lead troops in the field.

Lee first distinguished himself on the battlefield during the Mexican War in 1846. General Winfield Scott described Lee as "the very best soldier in the field."

CHAPTER

2

Mexico and Beyond

Trouble began with Mexico when American settlers moved into the northern part of the Mexican Republic. The new arrivals called the country they settled Texas, and they won their independence in a war with Mexico. After a few years, Texas became a part of the United States. From the beginning, Texans considered themselves a southern, slave-owning state, and they would later become a part of the Confederacy. In 1846, however, Mexico still insisted it owned part of the land that the Texans claimed was theirs. It was a conflict that was destined to lead to violence.

The residents of Texas claimed that the Rio Grande was the rightful southern boundary of their state. The Mexicans, however, insisted that Texas ended at the Nueces River, 130 miles north. President James Polk ordered the United States Army to occupy the disputed land. General Zachary Taylor led the American troops against the Mexicans, and there were several battles in which U.S. soldiers were killed. Finally, on May 13, Congress declared war on the Republic of Mexico. Before that, Lee had written to his wife, "I never could see the advantage to be gained by sending General Taylor unless it was to *invite* the Mexicans to attack." Lee told his wife it was a war that "we had not the frankness or manliness to declare." It would not be the last time that Lee protested against the connection between politics and war.

In August 1846, Lee was ordered to report to Texas. He arrived in San Antonio on September

21 and joined the staff of Brigadier General John Wool. Lee was just in time to march with 2,000 men against the Mexicans. General Wool's forces were part of a combined attack that the army expected would make Mexico quit the war. Lee helped the engineers find the best way through the rugged country they had to cross. It took a long time to catch up with the Mexican army. They were carefully avoiding the Americans.

After Christmas, Lee volunteered to serve as a scout. He rode quietly out of camp. When he returned several days later, he formed a *cavalry* unit to do more scouting. The next time he left, Lee found the enemy, and he was promoted to acting inspector general of Wool's army.

Lee was sent to the Gulf Coast in January 1847. There he reported to General Winfield Scott, who was preparing to assault Veracruz, a coastal fortress about 500 miles south of the Rio Grande. Lee was pleased to find that an old friend from West Point, Joe Johnston, was also on Scott's

General Zachary Taylor, also known as Old Rough and Ready, was another standout of the Mexican War. Taylor would later become the 12th president of the United States.

staff. The two shared a cabin on the flagship Massachusetts when the army of 6,000 sailed south.

It took almost three weeks to reach Veracruz. On March 5, Scott's flotilla was met by enemy warships on blockade duty. The American forces put troops ashore and landed their *artillery* batteries on the beach. Lee set the guns in position and directed the assault against the fortress town. On March 27, the city surrendered.

The next big target was Mexico City. It was far inland, and Scott's army marched toward it in mid-April. They crossed miles of sand heated by a scorching sun. The Americans were stopped at a fortified mountain pass. Lee proposed to General Scott that he be allowed to scout for a way around the enemy. Lee led a small party up the mountains. He lifted cannons by ropes and pulleys and got behind the defenders. Lee's batteries attacked the Mexican rear while General Scott launched an assault from the front. Some 3,000 prisoners were taken as the Americans stormed through the mountain passes. For his "coolness and gallantry" in combat, Lee was promoted to the rank of major.

Lee would soon be promoted again. He was made a lieutenant colonel for the key role he played in the capture of Mexico City. In that victorious assault, Lee had once more shown his skill as a scout and engineer. The Mexican general, the notorious Santa Anna who had massacred the Texas *garrison* at the Alamo, believed he was protected by a bed of hardened lava that blocked the American forces. Lee found a way through the tricky terrain for a backdoor assault. On September 13, General Scott's army captured Mexico City.

The commanding general wrote in his report that Lee's work was "the greatest feat of physical and moral courage performed by any individual." He called Lee the "very best soldier in the field" that he had ever seen. Lee had learned tactics by observing the way General Scott led his army. Fifteen years later, he would use what he had learned in the campaigns of the Civil War.

Lee also came to know almost every officer who would later lead armies on either side in the Civil War. Three of those whom he met in Mexico were especially important: George McClellan, who would be his first opponent; Ulysses S. Grant, who would ultimately defeat him; and Joseph Johnston, who would give over his command of Confederate troops to Lee in the midst of the Civil War.

In the years between the end of the Mexican War and the approaching war between the free and slave states, Lee's military life continued. His first assignment was to rebuild fortifications around Baltimore, Maryland. This meant he could be with his family again. The army let him be only a part-time father, but he wrote long and loving letters to his children from his army posts. He usually had a dog and cats, and he included amusing stories about his pets in his letters. During the times he could be with his family, Lee taught his sons how to hunt, shoot, and ride and shared his time affectionately with his daughters.

At one point Lee was offered the command of a revolutionary force that wanted to free Cuba from Spanish rule. He was tempted by the call to action—it seemed to be a just cause. However, it was fortunate for Lee that he turned it down. The attempt failed, and the leaders were shot by a firing squad.

Lee's next assignment was to be the superintendent of the U.S. Military Academy. Although this was a high honor, Lee was reluctant to accept. He longed for active duty. Still, in the summer of 1852, he took command of the academy from which he had been commissioned more than 20 years earlier. Things had changed at West Point. Almost all the buildings were new, and the old faculty was gone. However, one generation of cadets was much like another. One cadet was particularly familiar: Lee's eldest son, Custis, was a cadet. The older Lee had not wanted a military career for his son, but he accepted his

In 1852, the War Department ordered Lee to return to West Point as the academy's new superintendent. There he met James "Jeb" Stuart, an eager young cadet from Virginia who would later play an important part in the Civil War.

son's desire to follow the family tradition. Custis's cousin Fitzhugh was at the academy, too.

Colonel Lee served at West Point for three years. He was a good superintendent. He insisted on discipline, but the cadets knew they had a friend when one was needed. He kept a watchful eye on every cadet and hated most of all to send one home for failing. His wife, Mary, and their active young children liked the life at West Point, but the army once again found a new assignment for Lee. Jefferson Davis, who was to become the president of the Confederacy, was then the nation's secretary of war. Davis was also a West Pointer. He convinced Congress to provide the army with two new cavalry regiments, one of which would be led by Colonel Robert E. Lee. They were needed in Texas, where frontier duty was not much different than it had been 10 years earlier. Now, instead of chasing Mexican soldiers, Lee tracked Mexican bandits. The Comanche Indians resented the United States and its army, and raiding parties were frequently on the warpath.

In 1857, word reached Lee in San Antonio that his father-in-law, George Washington Parke Custis, had died. Lee was granted leave to go home and comfort his wife and to take care of her father's estate. A generous, kindly man, George Custis had let his property run down. Lee asked for additional leave to put the family fortunes in order. Years earlier, Lee had freed the slaves who came with the property in Arlington that Mary had inherited. Now he had to arrange for the freedom of his father-in-law's 200 slaves. A moral and compassionate man, Lee could neither sell other humans nor simply turn them out without the means to support themselves. It would be two full years before Lee had straightened out the Custis estate.

While he was on leave in Arlington, Lee was suddenly ordered to rush to Harpers Ferry, Virginia. The United States *arsenal* had been captured by John Brown, a fanatical opponent of slavery. Brown, his sons, and a few rebellious blacks were in control of the arsenal. Brown had earlier led an uprising in Kansas, and the government now feared that he would start a *revolt* among slaves in Virginia. Lee hurried to Harpers Ferry with a *detachment* of marines. They were led by a young lieutenant named Jeb Stuart. Later he would become famous for his cavalry raids against the Union armies. He would be one of Lee's greatest attack weapons. At Harpers Ferry he followed Lee's order to rush the roundhouse where Brown was garrisoned. In several minutes, the soldiers had overcome Brown and his men. Brown was tried for treason and hanged. But Brown's memory would prove harder to kill. He became a symbol of the protests against slavery. "John Brown's Body" became a marching song in the northern states.

Robert E. Lee was greatly disturbed that the North and South were being driven apart by politics. Orators on both sides aroused passions. Newspapers slanted opinion in either direction. Quietly, Lee turned the management of the family's estates over to his eldest son, Custis, who was now a lieutenant posted close by in Washington, D.C. Colonel Lee went back to his regiment in Texas. He sadly watched the nation get ready for war. First South Carolina, in December 1860, then six other states, including Texas, seceded from the Union. On February 4, 1861, Jefferson Davis was elected president of the Confederate States of America. The same day, Colonel Lee received orders to leave Texas and report to General Winfield Scott in Washington. General Scott asked Robert E. Lee to take command of the United States Army, and Lee resigned his commission.

Both sides expected the war to end quickly. President Lincoln put General George B. McClellan at the head of the Army of the Potomac. Its main responsibility was to defend the nation's capital on the banks of the Potomac River. General Lee named his forces the Army of Northern Virginia when he was given total command after early setbacks to southern armies. Although important battles would be fought as far west as the Mississippi River, much of the Civil War fighting took place in Virginia. The battles were fought between the Army of the Potomac and the Army of Northern Virginia. The capitals of the warring nations, Washington, D.C., and Richmond, Virginia, were only 100 miles apart. Both sides thought they could capture the other's major city and end the war.

Armies filled with eager recruits marched against each other. Troops paraded into battle in close formations. They pressed forward with flags flying and bands playing. The death tolls were awesome. At first everyone thought war was an exciting adventure. When the first combat took place at Bull Run, near Washington, D.C., ladies and their gentlemen escorts rode in carriages to see the event. The music stopped when the Confederates routed the raw Yankee recruits. The Union responded by taking the war seriously. It built up vast armies, produced guns, and stocked supplies. Soon Admiral Farragut captured New Orleans. General Ulysses S. Grant was victorious in Tennessee and Alabama. Western Virginia was soon in *Federal* hands. McClellan landed 115,000 fully equipped men east of Richmond, Virginia. They closed in on the Confederate capital. Faced with this mounting crisis, Confederate president Jefferson Davis turned the armies over to General Lee. Lee was clearly the finest military commander in the Confederate ranks. Could he now save Richmond and lead the Confederacy to victory?

Like Lee, Confederate president Jefferson Davis was a graduate of West Point and a veteran of the Mexican War. The two men were the key figures in the South's struggle for independence.

CHAPTER

3
Commanding the Army of Northern Virginia

Lee had 80,000 men in the Army of Northern Virginia. Most were Virginians, but regiments from other southern states were hurrying to Richmond. Young men from Louisiana, Georgia, and Texas, where Lee had served, came eager for battle. Lee would need every last one of them.

McClellan, with his 115,000 soldiers, was less than 10 miles from Richmond. Another large Federal army was coming through the Shenandoah Valley. Still another was poised to attack from Fredericksburg, only 50 miles north of Richmond.

Lee had learned a good lesson from General Winfield Scott in Mexico—the best thing to do when outnumbered is to attack. Instead of digging in, Lee went on the offensive. He used some of his forces to drive north and scatter the Union troops in the valley. With other soldiers he threatened the army at Fredericksburg. It pulled back to defend Washington, D.C. This left only McClellan for Lee to fight. Lee had another advantage. He knew McClellan was a cautious leader. It was easy to stay a jump ahead of an opponent who always waited until all conditions were favorable.

Even better for Lee, the general who had routed the armies north of Richmond was Stonewall Jackson. Jackson had received his unusual nickname from Lee at the first Battle of Manassas. When the rebels seemed ready to crack, Lee had

Confederate general Thomas "Stonewall" Jackson led his men to a number of important victories during the first two years of the war. He was fatally wounded by one of his own soldiers in 1863.

rallied them. "There stands Jackson, like a stone wall," he had declared. Now, having faked the northern forces into defending Washington, Jackson hurried to join Lee at Richmond.

General Lee now needed information. He called on Jeb Stuart, who took his cavalry and daringly rode clear around McClellan's forces. He reported back to Lee that the enemy was spread along the James River and the muddy waters of the Chickahominy below Richmond. With the Union army divided, Lee hammered away. He hit with a series of blows that would later be known as the Seven Days Campaign. McClellan's scattered army reeled in retreat. Lee gave his own exhausted army a brief rest. It had been well earned. With inferior numbers, Lee had beaten the largest army ever to take the field in America.

Lee could not rest long. McClellan still had 100,000 men to which he could soon add a new army division commanded by General John Pope. Lincoln had brought Pope from his command in the West to help with the siege of Richmond. Again, Lee knew his enemy. Pope was another general who took a lot of time getting ready to fight. Lee took the daring risk of splitting his army into two separate units. He gave half of his men to

Jackson, who returned to the valley. A native Virginian, Jackson knew the countryside; Pope did not. General Pope was tricked into thinking he was chasing Jackson. Actually, Stonewall Jackson had made Pope the *quarry*. At Manassas, where the South had won the first Battle of Bull Run, Jackson's forces sprang from a gap in the mountains. Then Lee came up and attacked from Pope's rear. It was a disaster for the North.

It had been only 10 weeks since Lee had been placed in command of the outnumbered Confederate forces. In that short period of time, he had routed McClellan's vast army. With the aid of Jackson, he had cleared the Shenandoah Valley of the forces led by General Pope. Lee had chased the Yankees out of Virginia. Instead of defending Richmond, he was now able to move against Washington, D.C.

Lee's men were a scruffy lot. Their uniforms were ragged and many were barefoot. They were scrawny and fed mostly on what they could find. Still, they marched with jaunty confidence. Lee led them boldly into enemy country, and they startled the North. Soon they were in Maryland and Pennsylvania, where Lee again divided his forces. He sent one division to capture the arsenal at Harpers Ferry. By bad luck, one of Lee's officers dropped a copy of the battle plan, and it somehow got into McClellan's hands. Even the timid McClellan could act decisively when he knew what his opponent was planning to do—particularly an enemy he outnumbered by two to one.

Wounded Confederate troops are treated by a doctor after the bloody Battle of Antietam, where more than 4,000 men were killed and 19,000 were wounded.

What followed in September 1862 was the bloodiest fighting of the war, the infamous Battle of Antietam. Lee's forces held high ground in the Maryland countryside. McClellan's men charged against them. The casualties on both sides were frightful. Lee rode up and down the lines on his gray charger, Traveller. He waved his sword and urged his troops to hold on. He hoped help would arrive in time. General A. P. Hill, who had attacked Harpers Ferry, was hurrying to Lee's aid. As the day was ending, a cloud of dust approached. It was Hill's men, running to the rescue. They never paused. They charged into the battle, screaming the rebel yell. The North's army faltered. Then they gave up and retreated toward Washington. The next night Lee withdrew to Virginia.

The assassination of President Abraham Lincoln in April 1865 dealt a tremendous blow to the Confederacy. Without Lincoln's leadership and commitment to unity, the southern states were severely punished by an angry U.S. Congress.

CHAPTER

4

The High Tide of the Confederacy

Once again the Northern cry "On to Richmond!" was heard along the northern Virginia countryside. Lincoln had now turned to General Ambrose E. Burnside to lead fresh armies against the capital of the South. In the winter of 1862–63, Burnside led 125,000 Union troops down the familiar road that led to Richmond. Lee chose the ground he would defend. The Confederate army dug trenches in the hills at Fredericksburg. Burnside believed that sheer numbers of troops would overpower an enemy. He was an *obstinate* man. He sent wave after wave of blue uniforms against the Confederates. They were shot down in sickening numbers. Four times, Union soldiers charged up that dreadful hill. They were finally withdrawn. Burnside was the latest Union general to underestimate Robert E. Lee.

   The North was not done yet. Next, President Lincoln turned to General Joseph Hooker, known to his men as Fighting Joe. The Union armies waited until the spring of 1863 to try again. It was the wrong time of year to attack Lee on his home ground. Early rains and melting snow made creeks overflow. The ground was muddy and the roads were impassable. Lee staked out a position at Chancellorsville in a place called the Wilderness. It was a dense forest, filled with thorny bushes. This did not seem to bother General Hooker. He had come spoiling for a fight. He had 140,000 fresh men. Lee had less than half as many.

Once again Lee split his smaller army in half. Stonewall Jackson took most of the men—28,000 footsore soldiers—on a sweep around Hooker's flank. Lee taunted Hooker with a smaller force of 14,000. When Hooker took the bait, Lee retreated into the Wilderness. Foolishly, Hooker followed. The Confederates, fighting on familiar ground, took a terrible toll on the enemy troops. Then Stonewall Jackson attacked. Jackson completely destroyed Hooker's exposed flank, and the Union army fled.

The Confederacy paid a bitter price for its victory, however. Battle action is always confusing. There is noise and movement, fear and excitement. Fighting among the trees and undergrowth of the Wilderness made it even harder to tell friend from foe. A Rebel patrol fired on what it thought was a Union raiding party. It was a mistake. On May 10, 1863, General Stonewall Jackson was accidentally killed by his own men. He would be badly missed by Lee, who now was ready to attack the North.

Lee believed that even with fewer men he could defeat the North. Still another Union general had been put in charge. General George G. Meade, another of Lee's comrades from the Mexican War, now led the Army of the Potomac. Lee divided his Army of Northern Virginia into three groups. General James "Old Pete" Longstreet was in charge of the first corps. General Richard Ewell, a cavalryman, led the second corps, and A. P. Hill headed the third corps. Lee boldly moved out of Virginia and into Pennsylvania. His troops were amazed to see fields filled with growing crops. They seized cattle and pigs and chickens. Next, needing shoes, they headed for Gettysburg, where they believed they would find a warehouse filled with boots. To the Rebels' surprise, the place was swarming with Union soldiers when A. P. Hill's troops arrived. Without expecting it, the Army of Northern Virginia had met the enemy.

For the first time, General Lee did not have a clear idea of what might happen. The once reliable Jeb Stuart had failed to return from a

Until the Battle of Gettysburg, Lee had consistently been able to overcome larger numbers of enemy troops through superior strategy and tactics. At Gettysburg, however, disorganization among Lee's generals led to uncoordinated attacks that allowed the Union soldiers to maintain the upper hand.

scouting mission. The cavalry leader was expected to tell Lee where the Union forces were. Forced to guess, Lee headed for Gettysburg. A battle was already going on when he got there. Hill's third corps was lined up against rows of Union troops. Suddenly, Ewell's second corps arrived and hit the Union flank. Lee seemed to have had an unexpected victory falling into his lap.

Victory appeared certain for the South when the Federal troops fled to the hills outside Gettysburg. Lee rushed to the top of Seminary Ridge to study the scene. South of the town, another ridge, with the similar name of Cemetery Ridge, had been left unoccupied. Lee sent word for General Ewell to get his troops in place before the Federal troops did. Nothing happened—Ewell froze. He had never had such a responsibility before.

The next day, General Longstreet also disappointed Lee. Instead of moving out against a thin line of Union defenders, he waited for one of his divisions to catch up with his main body. For hours he refused to attack. Meanwhile, the Union ranks were filling up with fresh troops rushed to the battle scene by General Meade. By the time Longstreet did advance, Cemetery Ridge was a Union fortress. Then, as Longstreet's assault sputtered out, General Ewell finally attacked from the north. Several *brigades* under General Jubal Early almost reached Meade's headquarters, but they were beaten off. The chance for a victory, which might have brought the collapse of the North, was gone—at least for the day.

That night, General Lee sat in his tent. He had lost 9,000 troops. Yet he still felt he could turn the tide of the war. Longstreet's final division, led by General George Pickett, had arrived. Longstreet argued that the attack should hit the middle of Meade's line. He wanted Pickett to lead the charge. Had an attack by Longstreet's first corps been launched promptly, the South might have won the Battle of Gettysburg. However, while

Longstreet and Pickett were insisting Lee do it their way, General Ewell got going. Lee had tried to delay him, but word did not get through in time. Instead, uncoordinated attacks were set in motion.

The Confederates had 140 cannons lined up wheel-to-wheel on Seminary Ridge. The cannons were fired at Union artillery positions on top of Cemetery Ridge. For two hours, the heaviest bombardment ever seen in battle in North America thundered. When the firing slowed down, 15,000 Confederate troops formed a line of three divisions. They advanced in a line that was more than a half mile wide and 1,000 men deep. The gray-clad divisions, the best of the unconquered Army of Northern Virginia, marched toward Cemetery Ridge.

The vast line of Confederate soldiers formed a target that the Union gunners on the ridge could not miss. Artillery barrages tore huge gaps in the Confederate ranks. When the survivors struggled on, Union riflemen, firing from behind a stone wall, shot them down. A few managed to get over the wall but were either killed or captured at once. General Lee rode down to meet the survivors of his army. With darkness coming on, the battlefield was silent. Only the moans of the wounded survivors were heard. That night, holding Traveller by the bridle, Lee cried out: "I never saw troops behave more magnificently than Pickett's division of Virginians did today in that grand charge upon the enemy. And if they had been supported as they were to have been . . . the day would have been ours."

Throughout the early years of the war, Lee was able to outsmart and outmaneuver one Union general after another. The North's luck suddenly changed, however, when President Lincoln appointed Ulysses S. Grant, shown here, to head the Union army.

CHAPTER

5
The Defeat of the South

On July 3, 1863, the South suffered two decisive losses. Lee was defeated at Gettysburg; and in the West, Vicksburg, Mississippi, surrendered to General Ulysses S. Grant. The gray-bearded General Lee led his weary troops back to Virginia. His ambitions to capture Washington were over. Now it would take all his cleverness to protect Richmond.

The summer and fall months passed, and Lee set up his camp for the winter. Grant had continued to overwhelm the Confederate forces in the West. The Union general broke a Confederate siege at Chattanooga and appeared to be headed for Georgia. Jefferson Davis called on Lee to head him off, but the Virginian wanted to protect Richmond, his own state's largest city. President Lincoln put General Grant in charge of all the North's armies. On March 24, 1864, Grant began the final campaign to end the bloody war. The North was greatly superior in manpower and supplies. The forceful Grant pressed on toward Richmond. General William Tecumseh Sherman marched on Atlanta, Georgia, leaving a wide path of devastation across the South.

On May 4, Grant marched 120,000 men toward Richmond. Lee had 70,000 men. To Lee's delight, Grant headed toward the Wilderness. This was where General Hooker had blundered the year before. However, Grant's soldiers fought the Rebels in tough hand-to-hand combat. Even though the South lost a great number of men, they did not back off. The two generals, Grant and

Lee, maneuvered against each other. Each time Grant headed for Richmond, Lee guessed right and headed him off. But each time the armies fought, Lee lost men he could not replace. Grant could always fill his ranks with fresh troops.

Lee suffered massive losses in both quantity and quality. General Longstreet was wounded by a Confederate bullet in the Wilderness. General Hill collapsed from nervous exhaustion. General Stuart went down before a Federal cavalry raid. Lee himself suffered intestinal pains and could not ride Traveller. He was forced to command his troops from the back of an ambulance.

At Cold Harbor, only 10 miles northeast of Richmond, the two armies faced each other again at the beginning of June. Lee beat back a frontal assault that cost Grant 7,000 men in less than an hour. Then, learning that the Union general, Philip Sheridan, was advancing down the Shenandoah Valley, Lee sent General Early with 8,000 men to head him off. Lee could not risk having Sheridan's forces join with Grant's. Lee had only 28,000

Confederate troops await an attack from Union soldiers in reinforced bunkers at Fort Mahone in Virginia. After Lee's troops were defeated at Gettysburg, they were forced to return to Richmond to defend the Confederate capital from the advancing Union army.

infantry men left, and those tattered forces were starving and almost out of bullets. Grant wanted to cut the last railroad line that could still bring supplies to Richmond. The two armies faced each other at Petersburg. If Grant won there, he could starve Richmond into finally giving up.

Lee's faint hopes were pinned on General Early's small force in the Shenandoah Valley. Although they were greatly outnumbered, Early's soldiers chased the Union troops up into the hills. Then they dashed toward Washington. Some of Early's troops actually got close enough to see Abraham Lincoln nervously watching from the top of Union fortifications. Then General Grant sent his reserves to the rescue. They chased Early's small band away.

Meanwhile, Lee managed to gather 50,000 men in trenches at Petersburg. Many of the replacements had retreated from battles lost on other fronts. Even with the reinforcements, the Confederate forces faced twice as many Union troops under Grant. The hot summer weather made things worse for the Confederates. They had only rotten meat and uncooked grain to eat. They drank dirty water that spread *typhoid fever*. The siege at Petersburg went on through the autumn. Lee's men were deserting in great numbers. Some tried to get home for Christmas. Those who stayed suffered through a bitter, cold winter. There were so few Rebels in the trenches that they had to be placed 20 feet apart. Finally, on March 2, 1864, General Lee wrote a letter to his enemy, General Grant. He said he wished "to leave nothing untried which may put an end to the calamities of war." Grant told Lee that only President Lincoln could stop the war.

General Lee met with the Confederate president, Jefferson Davis, in Richmond. They could do one of three things: Lee could surrender; he could make a surprise attack on Grant; or, when the roads dried, Lee could head south. He could link up with the 15,000 troops that his old friend, General Joseph Johnston, led in North Carolina. Davis did not want to stop fighting unless the

North recognized the independence of the South. That, however, would mean the slaves who had been set free by Lincoln would no longer be free men. On January 1, 1863, Lincoln had announced that they no longer belonged to their Confederate masters. But only the Confederacy's defeat would guarantee this.

Desperate to change the course of the war, Lee attacked Grant. He tried to divide the North's armies but failed badly. His men no longer had the ability to fight in the field. Lee's only thought now was to spare the Army of Northern Virginia from further suffering. President Davis fled Richmond. General Lee asked General Grant to meet him at a private home in the town of Appomattox Courthouse, Virginia. On April 9, 1865, Lee, wearing his finest gray uniform, arrived riding Traveller. He waited for Grant. The Union general, dressed in muddy boots and the uniform he wore in battle, joined him.

The two generals respected each other. Grant was a gracious and thoughtful victor. He

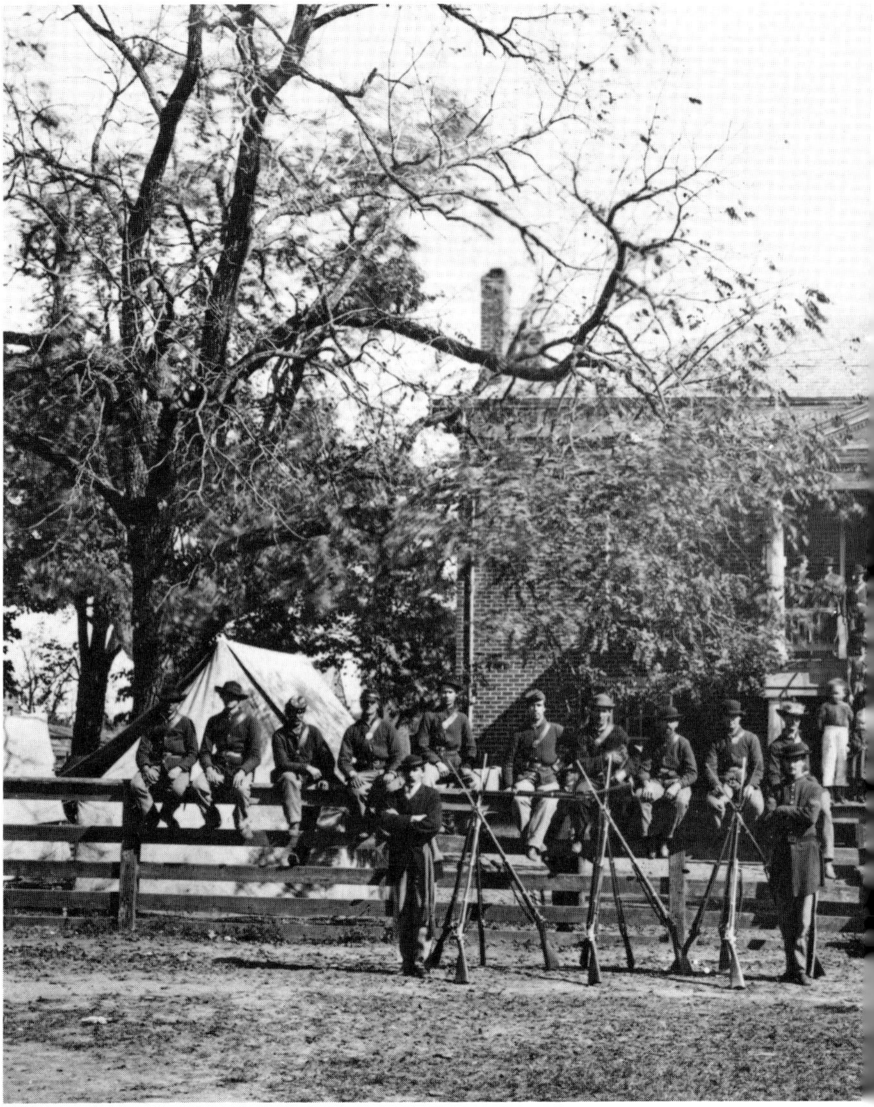

By the time Lee and Grant negotiated the Confederate surrender at Appomattox Courthouse, Lee's once-proud army had dwindled to a starving, exhausted group of soldiers dressed in ragged, bloodstained uniforms.

allowed Lee's men to keep any horses or mules that they owned. The animals would be needed for farm work. When Lee said that he held Union prisoners and asked for *rations* to feed them, Grant issued enough food for the soldiers on both sides. Defeat was difficult for Lee to accept, but General Grant made it as easy as possible. When the surrender was signed, Lee mounted Traveller and rode back to his camp. His weary troops cheered him as he went by. Lee held his head high. He knew that he had done everything that he could. He told his soldiers, "Men, we have fought the war together, and I have done the best I could for you."

On April 11, Lee wrote his final report as commanding general. The next day, Lee's troops surrendered their guns and battle flags in a formal ceremony. Three days later, Lee rode into Richmond. Members of his family waited for him at the house they had rented in the bombed-out city. On that same day, in Washington, D.C., President Abraham Lincoln was killed. An *assassin,* John

Wilkes Booth, shot and killed the president in a Washington theater. The nation, on the brink of *reunification,* was stunned.

Robert E. Lee remained in Richmond, recovering from his last campaign. He was saddened by the news of Lincoln's death. A wise and compassionate man, Lincoln had wanted to heal the wounds left by the war. Instead, a spiteful Congress passed laws to punish the South. Some members of Congress even wanted to put General Lee on trial for treason. General Grant said he would resign as commander of the army if they tried to do this. In response to Grant's threat, all charges against Lee were dropped.

Lee is pictured here after the war with his sons Custis (left) and Robert junior. When the fighting finally ended, the aging general was threatened with charges of treason by the United States Senate.

CHAPTER

6
After the War

Robert E. Lee was given his choice of many jobs when the war ended. Most of these would have been honorary positions. Lee would only have been expected to allow others to use his name to raise money or gain prestige for their institutions. Lee did not want that type of honorary position. He had no wish to profit from his wartime reputation as a hero. Too many men had died for him to do that.

Finally there came an offer that suited him perfectly. He was offered the presidency of a small college in Lexington, Virginia. Washington Col-

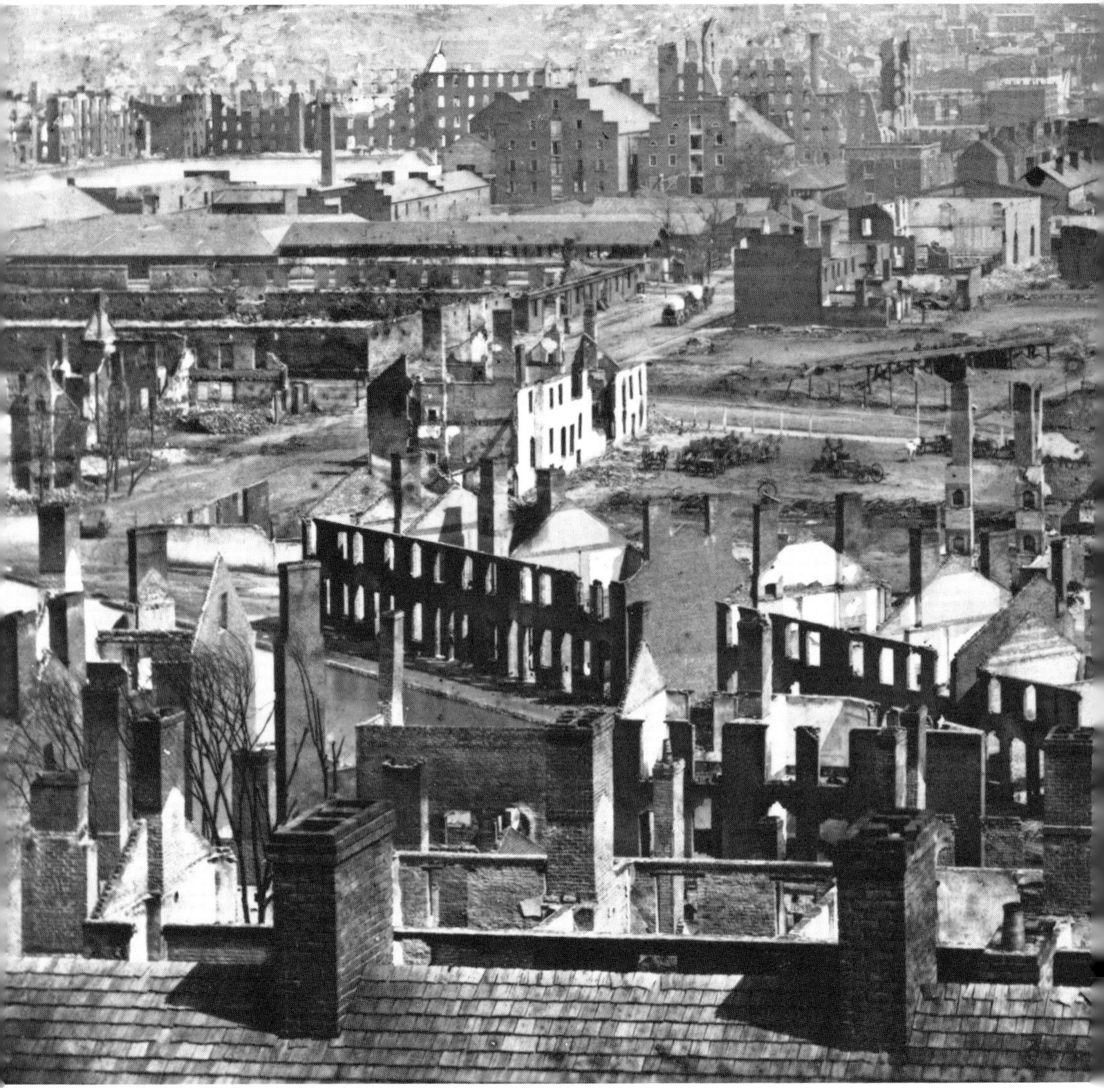

After the war, the Confederate capital of Richmond lay in ruins, along with much of the rest of the region. Lee and other survivors were faced with the task of rebuilding their homes and their communities.

lege was the sixth oldest in the nation. George Washington had endowed it in 1796. By the end of the Civil War, the school had been reduced to only a handful of 17-year-old students and four teachers who were too old to fight. Most of the buildings had been destroyed. Lexington was in the path of the action that had raged through the Shenandoah Valley.

It was just the right job for Lee. He used his skills as an engineer to rebuild the campus. His experience as superintendent at West Point also came in handy. Lee strongly believed that education of young people would help the South recover from the war. He changed the courses the college taught, adding classes in business, banking, and agriculture. When Lee moved his family into a house on the campus, his wife and their daughters found that everything had been provided by the townspeople. They sat down to a full breakfast served by welcoming neighbors. Every room was furnished. Every need had been met.

Each day during his tenure as president of Washington College, Lee rode his faithful horse, Traveller, through the streets of Lexington, Virginia. Residents reported that the retired general followed such a strict schedule that they could set their watches by his comings and goings.

Lee rode Traveller daily through the streets of Lexington. People said they could set their clocks by his regular rounds throughout the town. He was always punctual—always on schedule. He realized that he still had much to do as he began the final stage of his life. He looked 10 years older than his 58 years. His gray beard was a sign that he had been severely aged by the war years. However, he was able to enjoy five productive years as president of the college. Before he died on October 12, 1870, the school had grown from 40 students to 400. The most impressive of the school's new buildings was the chapel. It was completed in time for graduation exercises in 1868. Lee attended daily worship services with his students in the chapel auditorium. His own office was in a room at the lower level. The room can be seen today, just as Lee left it for the last time in 1870. Soon after his death, the trustees changed the name of the school to Washington and Lee University. The chapel became, in part, a museum to both generals. It is also the tomb of General Robert E. Lee and his family. The remains of Lee's beloved horse, Traveller, are buried just outside the building.

Lee's estates in Arlington, Virginia, have been turned into the Arlington National Cemetery. It is the final resting place for many of America's heroes. President John F. Kennedy is buried there, and the Tomb of the Unknowns is located among the cemetery's rolling hills.

Robert E. Lee left a great legacy for those who followed him. He was one of history's finest military leaders, but he was also a great human being. He was a devoted husband and father and a skilled educator. Though he lost the greatest battle of his life, he always remained true to his ideals. For that, he earned the respect of both his friends and his enemies.

Further Reading

Brown, Warren. *Robert E. Lee.* New York: Chelsea House, 1992.

Casdorph, Paul D. *Lee and Jackson.* New York: Dell, 1992.

Commager, Henry S., and Lynd Ward. *America's Robert E. Lee.* Boston: Houghton Miflin, 1963.

Freeman, Douglas Southall. *Lee.* New York: Scribners, 1961.

Kantor, MacKinlay. *Lee and Grant at Appomattox.* New York: Random House, 1950.

Long, A. L. *Memoirs of Robert E. Lee.* Secaucus, NJ: Blue and Grey Press, 1983.

Smith, Gene. *Lee and Grant.* New York: Meridian, 1985.

Vinton, Iris. *The Story of Robert E. Lee.* New York: Grosset & Dunlap, 1952.

Wilson, Douglas. *The Civil War.* New York: Galahad, 1982.

Glossary

arsenal   storage place for guns, ammunition, and war supplies

artillery   large guns that are mounted on wheels or tracks because they are too heavy to carry

assassin   a murderer, especially one who kills an important person

besieged   surrounded by troops

brigade   a large army unit

cadet   a student at a military school

cavalry   troops trained to fight on horseback

commission   rank granted to a military officer

detachment   troops selected from a larger unit

Federals   Union soldiers

garrison   a military base or the troops stationed at a military base

infantry   troops trained to fight on foot

insurrection   the act of rebelling against an established government

obstinate   stubbornly holding to an attitude or opinion

prominent   widely known

quarry   one that is sought or pursued

rations   food issued in times of scarcity

reunification   the act of bringing back together again

revolt   a renouncing of loyalty, often expressed in a rebellion or uprising

secede   to withdraw formally

typhoid fever   a very serious contagious disease that is marked by high fever and is caused by germs in dirty food or water

Union   the United States of America

Chronology

1807   Robert Edward Lee is born at Stratford Hall, Westmoreland County, Virginia, on January 19

1810   Lee family is forced to leave Stratford and moves to Alexandria, Virginia

1825–29   Lee attends U.S. Military Academy at West Point; graduates second in class

1831   Marries Mary Custis

1846   Sent to Mexico in August to fight in Mexican War

1852   Named superintendent of U.S. Military Academy at West Point

1859   John Brown is hanged after Lee captures him at Harpers Ferry

1861   First southern states begin to secede from the Union in January; Confederates attack Fort Sumter in April; Civil War begins; Lee resigns from U.S. Army; First Battle of Manassas in July; Lee sent to western Virginia to coordinate Confederate defense

1862   Lee named commander in chief of Confederate forces by President Jefferson Davis; Second Battle of Manassas in August; Battle of Antietam in September

1863   Lincoln frees southern slaves with the Emancipation Proclamation on January 1; Battle of Gettysburg July 1–3; Ulysses S. Grant takes command of U.S. Army of the Potomac on March 24

1864   Battle of the Wilderness May 5–6; siege of Petersburg begins on June 18

1865   Lee begins final retreat of the Army of Northern Virginia on April 2; he surrenders to Grant at Appomattox Courthouse on April 9; President Lincoln is assassinated on April 15; Lee becomes president of Washington College in Lexington, Virginia, in September

1870   Lee dies in Lexington on October 12

1975   Lee's citizenship restored by U.S. House of Representatives

INDEX

Antietam, Battle of, 39–41,
Arlington, Virginia, 16, 71
Army of Northern Virginia, 31, 35, 46, 50, 59
Army of the Potomac, 31, 46

Brown, John, 29–30
Bull Run, Battle of, 32, 39
Burnside, Ambrose E., 43, 44

Calhoun, John C., 13
Chancellorsville, Battle of, 44–45
Civil War, 7, 24, 25, 31–62, 68
Cold Harbor, Battle of, 55
Confederate States of America, 7, 8–9, 10, 19, 31
Custis, George Washington Parke, 16, 28–29

Davis, Jefferson, 28, 31, 33, 54, 58, 59

Early, Jubal, 49, 55, 57
Ewell, Richard, 46, 48, 49, 50

Fredericksburg, Battle of, 43–44

Gettysburg, Battle of, 46–51, 53
Grant, Ulysses S., 25, 32, 53, 54, 57, 58, 59, 62, 63

Harper's Ferry, Virginia, 29–30
Hill, A. P., 41, 46, 48, 55
Hooker, Joseph, 44, 45, 54

Jackson, Stonewall, 36, 37, 39, 45
"John Brown's Body," 30
Johnston, Joseph, 21, 25, 58

Lee, Custis (son), 26, 30
Lee, Mary Custis (wife), 15, 16, 20, 28, 68
Lee, Anne Carter, (mother) 12, 15
Lee, Henry ("Light-Horse Harry"), 9(father), 9, 12
Lee, Robert E.,
    birth, 10
    and John Brown's raid, 29–30
    childhood, 10–11

as commander of the Army of Northern Virginia, 33, 35–62
death, 70
education, 12–13
engineering career, 15, 24, 68
marriage, 16
and Mexican War, 20–25, 36
as president of Washington College, 65–70
as superintendent of U.S. Military Academy, 26–28, 68
surrender at Appomattox Courthouse, 58–62
Lexington, Virginia, 65, 68, 70
Lincoln, Abraham, 8, 31, 43, 44, 54, 57, 58, 59, 62, 63
Longstreet, James, 46, 48, 49, 55

McClellan, George, 25, 31, 32, 36, 38, 39, 41
Manassas, battles of, 39
Meade, George G., 46, 49
Mexican War, 19–25, 36, 46
Military Academy, U.S., 12, 15, 26, 28

Pickett, George, 49, 51
Petersburg, Siege of, 57–58
Pope, John, 38, 39

Richmond, Virginia, 32, 35, 36, 37, 38, 39, 43, 53, 54, 55, 58, 59, 62, 63

Scott, Winfield, 10, 21, 23, 31, 36
Seven Days Campaign, 38
Sherman, William Tecumseh, 54
Stuart, Jeb, 30, 38, 46, 55

Taylor, Zachary, 20
Traveller, 41, 51, 55, 59, 62, 70, 71

War of 1812, 13
Washington and Lee College. *See* Washington College
Washington College, 65-70
Washington, George, 9, 12
West Point. *See* Military Academy,
U.S. Wilderness, battle of, the 54–55
Wool, John, 21

Jack Kavanagh began his freelance writing career as a high school correspondent for the *Brooklyn Eagle* in the 1930s. He has served as a contributing editor to *Sports History,* and his work has appeared in magazines such as *Sports Heritage, Vine Line,* and *Diversions.* He is the author of several books for young people, including *Honus Wagner, Grover Cleveland Alexander,* and *Rogers Hornsby* for Chelsea House's BASEBALL LEGENDS series. Mr. Kavanagh lives in North Kingston, Rhode Island.

Eugene C. Murdoch, a professor of history at Marietta College in Ohio, published one of the most complete bibliographies about the Civil War. He was the president of the Society for American Baseball Research and wrote a biography of Ban Johnson, the first president of the American League. Mr. Murdoch died in 1992.

Picture Credits

The Bettmann Archive: pp. 14, 64; Mathew Brady Studio, Library of Congress: pp. 6 (neg. #B8172-1), 27 (neg. #B-8184-10375), 60–61 (neg. #B8184-7193); Alexander Gardner, The Bettmann Archive: pp. 66–67; Alexander Gardner, Library of Congress: pp. 40 (neg. #B8171-588), 42 (neg. #USZ62-13016); Ernest L. Ipsen, Library of Congress: p. 18 (neg. #USZ62-8327); Library of Congress: pp. 34 (neg. #USZ62-38087), 47, 56 (neg. #B8171-1091), 69 (neg. #USZ62-10805), p. 11 (from a painting by A. Chappel; neg. #USZ62-49736); Timothy O'Sullivan, Library of Congress: p. 52 (neg. #B8184-B-36); John Sartain, Library of Congress: p. 22 (neg. #USZ62-7559); Courtesy of the Virginia State Library and Archives: p. 37; William E. West, Library of Congress: p. 2 (neg. #USZ62-21849).